PETER PAUL RUBENS

PETER PAUL RUBENS

FROUKJE HOEKSTRA

PARK
LANE

Cover illustrations

- The Fur Cloak, 1636-39 (detail)
  Vienna, Kunsthistorisches Museum
- The Flemish Fair, c. 1636
  Paris, The Louvre

First published in Great Britain in 1994
by Grange Books PLC
The Grange, Grange Yard, London SE1 3AG

This edition produced in co-operation with Arcturus Publishing Ltd.

Translated from the Dutch by Tony Langham and Plym Peters

Coordination and production: VBI/Smeets, Weert
Filmset: Zspiegel grafische zetterij, Best, The Netherlands
Print: Royal Smeets Offset b.v., Weert, The Netherlands

© Royal Smeets Offset b.v., Weert, The Netherlands

ISBN 1 85627 667 8

PETER PAUL RUBENS

Peter Paul Rubens was born on 28 June 1577 in Siegen in the former German principality of Nassau, and died in Antwerp on 30 May 1640. The Flemish painter, drawer and diplomat was the son of Maria Pypelincks and Jan Rubens, a lawyer and alderman of Antwerp, who had fled to Germany because of his Protestant beliefs. A year after his birth the family moved to Cologne. In 1589, two years after his father's death, Maria and her sons, Peter Paul and Philip returned to Antwerp, where Rubens went to the Latin school and then for a time became a page at Court of the Countess Ligne. From 1592 to 1598, he was apprenticed to Otto van Veen (Vaenius) amongst others, and in 1598, he was registered as a master in the Saint Lucas Guild in Antwerp. Two years later he travelled to Italy, where he spent eight years (in Mantua, Venice, Florence, Genoa and Rome). In Italy, Rubens studied classical sculpture, Renaissance painting and the work of contemporaries such as Caravaggio. In 1603, he spent some time at the Court in Madrid working on an official commission for King Philip III of Spain.

Following his return to Antwerp in 1608, Rubens was appointed the official city painter and he became the painter at the Court of the Archduke Albrecht and Archduchess Isabella. In 1609, he married Isabella Brant, who died in 1626; in 1630, he married Hélène Fourment. The artist, the "father" of Flemish Baroque, was exceptionally productive in his Antwerp studio and had a great influence on other painters with whom he often collaborated. In addition, he was a favourite of Isabella's; from 1623, she sent him abroad on important diplomatic missions. As a diplomat, he visited the great courts of Europe, where he was also valued as a painter and received important commissions.

To the general public, Rubens is known particularly as a painter of exuberant scenes, with many voluptuous - often naked - women. However, this artist's oeuvre was not only extensive, but was also exceptionally varied. The most important subjects of this Baroque creator of genius included altarpieces, portraits, mythological works, hunting scenes and landscapes. Even in his lifetime, he had a considerable international reputation.

Rubens' son, Nicolaas, 1625 - 1627
Red and black chalk, highlighted with white
29.2 x 23.2 cm
Vienna, Graphische Sammlung Albertina

A FAMILY IN EXILE

The history of the Rubens family is curiously interwoven with a decisive period in the history of the Netherlands. It was a time of great religious conflict: the Counter Revolution, the Eighty Years' War, and Alva's reign of terror. Tens of thousands of Flemish people left their country, which was ruled by the Spanish, in fear of being persecuted by the Inquisition because of their different Protestant beliefs. Rubens' parents also fled to Cologne in 1568 for this reason. (His father, Jan, was sympathetic to Calvinism, and later became a Lutheran.) The lawyer, Jan Rubens, who had been an alderman of Antwerp, became the legal advisor to Anna of Saxony, the second wife of Prince William of Orange. The rather shameless, twenty-six-year old Anna took the handsome young Rubens as her lover, and this almost cost him his head when, after a few years, the Prince discovered the relationship. In 1571, Rubens' father disappeared into the dungeon of the castle of Dillenburg awaiting the death penalty, which was the punishment for adultery. Following the countless pleading letters which Maria Rubens sent to the Prince, and probably also because William of Orange wished to avoid a public scandal, the punishment was mitigated in 1573 to exile in Siegen, in modern Westphalia.

Peter Paul (also known as Petrus Paulus and Pieter Paul) was born in 1577 in this town, in what was then the principality of Nassau. He was the sixth and penultimate child of Maria and Jan Rubens. A year later, the family was allowed to return to Cologne, where Rubens spent his childhood and of which he had fond memories. Towards the end of his life in 1637, he wrote in a letter that he felt a great deal of affection for the city of Cologne because he had grown up there until he was ten years old, and often wished to see the city again after all those years. However, he never did. Jan Rubens who had established a flourishing legal practice and had been converted to Catholicism, probably at his wife's insistence, died in 1587. Two years after his death, when Rubens was twelve years old, Maria Rubens returned to Antwerp with three of the surviving children, her daughter Blandina, who was about twenty years old, Peter Paul, and his brother, Philip, who was about three years older. The oldest brother, Jean Baptiste, was already an adult and was studying in Italy, where he died a few years later.

APPRENTICESHIP IN ANTWERP

When the fatherless family returned, the city of Antwerp had changed and become unrecognizable in the twenty years of Rubens' exile. The Duke of Alva's reign of terror, which had raged since 1566, had soon claimed hundreds of victims and had led to great revolt in the Netherlands. The Northern Netherlands, united under the leadership of William of Orange, concluded a treaty of independence in 1579. The Southern Netherlands were less fortunate. In 1576 the demoralized Spanish army mutinied, and during the "Spanish Fury", the prosperous houses of Antwerp were plundered, the city centre went up in flames and tens of thousands of people died. Half of the inhabitants of this once powerful port fled, before the hated Spanish troops finally left the city in 1577. For a time, the south joined the northern provinces in the battle against Spain, but this union was short-lived. In 1585, Antwerp capitulated to the Spanish army after a long seige, and the Southern Netherlands remained under Spanish dominion for another hundred and fifty years. As a result of this capitulation, sailors from Holland and Zeeland blockaded the mouth of the River Scheldt, so that no ships could enter or leave the port of Antwerp. The most powerful trading port in Europe was paralysed and had fallen into decay when the Rubens family returned, and it took a long time to recover.

The twelve-year-old Rubens went to the Latin school of Rombout Verdonck in this city. The latter continued the education of the intelligent boy, which Jan Rubens had started, and taught him classical languages and literature. At school, Rubens met Balthasar Moretus, the grandson of Christoffel Plantijn, who later established the famous printers. Moretus, who was a good friend of Rubens throughout his life, wrote about this, many years later: "I had known him since childhood and I loved this young man who had a perfect character and extremely friendly nature."

However, after two years Rubens had to leave school. His sister was getting married and the last of the family's money went towards her dowry. From that moment Peter Paul and Philip had to earn their own keep. Philip became a teacher, and continued his studies, and his younger brother became a page for the Countess Lalaing, Marguerite de Ligne-Arenberg, the widow of the former governor of Antwerp. Rubens probably owed this desirable position to his father's contacts with the nobility, and it is possible that his talent for drawing surfaced at court. Rubens himself never said anything about the reasons which led to his decision to become a painter, but it hardly seemed a coincidence that he left the Countess's Court after only a few months to be apprenticed to the landscape painter, Tobias Verhaecht.

Virtually nothing is known about Rubens' apprenticeship, except that he worked in the studios of Verhaecht, Adam van Noort and Otto van Veen (Octave Vaenius) between 1592 and 1598. All three were minor masters with no style of their own. Van Noort and Van Veen were so-called "historical" painters, which means that they painted mainly scenes from religious and world literature. Since the Renaissance, this form of painting had been considered to be the highest artistic expression and, moreover, the most intellectual, because the painter needed a thorough knowledge of both religious texts and classical and contemporary literature. The most important of the three teachers was Van Veen, with whom Rubens also worked once he had been enrolled as a master. Van Veen was a Romanist, a painter who had been to Rome to study the art of Antiquity and the Renaissance, and his work revealed a strong Italian influence. Following his example, Rubens left for Italy in 1600, two years after being enrolled in the Saint Lucas Guild of Painters in Antwerp.

COURT PAINTER IN ITALY

Only a few of Rubens' works as a young painter in his first independent years are known. One of these was *Adam and Eve*. However, he must have made an impression as a good painter, because when he was introduced to the Duke of Mantua, Vincenzo I Gonzaga, by a nobleman in Venice, Rubens was appointed court painter. This was a great honour, considering the reputation of the Duke's court as an artistic centre, where, since the fifteenth century, painters such as Mantegna, Bellini, Titian, Correggio and Tintoretto had created masterworks, which are still included amongst the greatest collections of paintings in the largest European and American museums. In fact, Gonzaga was not only interested in painting. Famous architects were working for the state, and when Rubens arrived in Mantua, Claudio Monteverdi was the court composer. The Duke had another court painter from the same city as Rubens, Frans Pourbus II, who was commissioned to prepare a gallery of portraits of "the most beautiful women of the world" for the Duke, who was as fond of women as he was of art. Apart from painting the portraits of the Duke's family and of "beautiful women" - which the painter did not seem to consider particularly important - one of Rubens' main tasks was to copy the famous old Italian masters. To do this, Gonzaga sent him to

Rome in 1601, where he was requested by a subsequent patron, the Archduke Albrecht, to paint an altarpiece for one of the seven traditional pilgrimage churches in the city, the Santa Croce de Gerusalemme. It was a mark of particular esteem for the young painter that he was given this important commission - his first major commission - and that his patron was more than satisfied. The triptych - *Saint Helena with the Cross*, *The Mockery of Jesus* and *The Elevation of the Cross*, which Rubens painted entirely in an Italian style, immediately became one of the most popular works of art.

While he stayed in Rome, Rubens copied many works for Gonzaga, but also for himself. He continued to do this throughout his time in Italy, and did countless sketches of famous classical sculptures. He studied the dynamics of Michelangelo, the compositions of Raphael, the use of colour of Titian and the brilliant effects of light (chiaroscuro or clair-obscur, which also influenced Rembrandt) of Caravaggio, who still lived in Rome at that time. He combined all these essential elements of the Renaissance masters in a new form, which was later known as Baroque.

THE YOUNG DIPLOMAT

In 1602, Rubens was back in Mantua, but less than a year later he left again and was away for a long time. The Duke entrusted him with a diplomatic mission to the court of King Philip III of Spain. Rubens had to accompany a large number of valuable gifts for the king, his powerful minister, the Duke of Lerma, and other leading courtiers. Gonzaga sent Rubens because he was in favour with Albrecht, Philip's son-in-law, and it would undoubtedly make a good impression. At the Spanish court, the twenty-six-year old painter revealed himself to be the diplomat he was later to become officially. During the four-week journey through Spain it rained constantly, and as a result, a number of the copies of Raphael's work which were meant for the Duke of Lerma were badly damaged. At first, Rubens refused to restore the paintings himself "My principles forbid me from combining my work with that of someone else, no matter how great", he argued. However, he eventually abandoned his principles, and the grateful Duke thought he had been sent genuine Raphaels, which Rubens - diplomatically - did not dispute. He was then commissioned to paint a portrait of the Duke of Lerma on horseback. This was a daring composition in which, for the first time, he used the dynamic upward, swirling movements which were to be become characteristic of much of his work.

At the beginning of 1604, Rubens returned to Mantua, where he worked until the end of 1605. It was during this period that he completed the Duke's biggest commission, a triptych for the Church of Santa Trinita in Mantua, with the centrepiece, *The Gonzaga Family's Adoration of the Holy Trinity* (a work which was cut into pieces by Napoleon's looting officers in 1797, after which the fragments were dispersed). Rubens then left for Genoa to paint an altarpiece for the Jesuit Church, *The Circumcision of Jesus*, as well as portraits of the nobility. From Genoa, he travelled back to Rome to copy paintings for the Duke, but while he was there he also accepted other commissions. He lived with his older brother, Philip, a follower of the humanist Justus Lipsius, the librarian for Cardinal Colonna, who introduced him to some very influential figures. Apart from a short interruption in 1607 when he went to Genoa for a time, Rubens spent the rest of his time in Italy in Rome, where he also studied architecture and archaeology.

As he wrote to the secretary of the Duke of Mantua at the end of 1606, he probably owed the best commission a painter in Rome could have dreamed of at that time to his contacts amongst the nobility. This was the commission for the painting for the high altar of the Church of the Oratoria, the Santa Maria della Vallicella or "Chiesa Nuova". This commission took him longer than he expected, because when the large canvas, *The Saints, Gregory the Great, Domitilla, Maurus and Papianus adoring the "Madonna della Vallicella"* or *The Vision of Saint Gregory*, was placed on the altar, it proved to be virtually invisible because the canvas reflected the incoming light. Rubens saw the painting and did a new version, this time a triptych on slate, which can still be admired in the church today. The work was completed in the autumn of 1608. Shortly afterwards, the painter heard that his mother was seriously ill and left for Antwerp immediately, without attending the unveiling of the altarpiece, and without waiting for permission from the Duke of Mantua. Although he wrote to the Duke's secretary that he would not be away long, Rubens never returned to Italy.

A FAVOURABLE CLIMATE

When Rubens arrived in Antwerp at the end of 1608, his mother had already died. In 1610, Rubens had the painting which he had done for the Chiesa Nuova placed above her grave in Saint Michael's Abbey, in posthumous homage. He undoubtedly considered returning to Italy where he had influential patrons, but in the end he decided to settle in Antwerp. Perhaps the fact that the relationship between him and the Duke of Mantua had cooled, because Gonzaga did not pay him promptly, contributed to this decision. It was certainly of great importance to the continued development of Flemish painting. However, the improvement of conditions in Antwerp was probably the decisive factor.

Shortly after Rubens' return the Twelve Years' Truce was signed and this encouraged the city's recovery, which was supported and financially aided by the policy of Archduke Albrecht, who ruled over the Southern Netherlands from 1598. One important aspect of the policy of the Spanish-Hapsburg dominion was the restoration and reconstruction of churches, monasteries and abbeys which had suffered great damage during the Iconoclastic Revolt, and the looting during the Spanish Fury. This resulted in an incredible number of commissions for artists in Antwerp. In addition, the blockade of the Scheldt by Holland had resulted in an agreement which meant that high freight tolls had to be paid. This led to a new trade in expensive luxury articles, especially objets d'art on which there was a greater profit margin, despite the toll. Because of this development, Antwerp was a leading city in the art trade in Europe in the seventeenth century. One factor was that the interest in objets d'art as investments and for speculation rapidly grew in Antwerp because the price of land and houses had considerably fallen in value following years of war and revolt. Altogether, it was an extremely positive atmosphere for artists.

SUCCESS IN ANTWERP

Albrecht and Isabella, who had already tried to attract Rubens as court painter in 1607, appointed him to this position in September 1609 and paid him a good annual salary. Rubens kept the title and the annual salary until his death. In addition, he was given exemption from the guild and city taxes, was given leave to continue doing commissions for others, and did not have to settle in the city of residence, Brussels.

Two weeks after obtaining his position as court painter, Rubens married the eighteen-year-old Isabella Brant, the elegant and intelligent daughter of an Antwerp lawyer and alderman. It was a good match, which lasted for seventeen years, and was overshadowed only by the early death of the eldest of their three children, Clara Serena, who was born in 1611 and died at the age of twelve. The resemblance between mother and daughter is clear from a comparison of the magnificent *Head of a Girl* (1616) and the portrait of the recently married couple dating from 1609. A year after his marriage, Rubens bought a property on the Wapper in the centre of Antwerp which he extended, adding a large studio. From that time, a large number of apprentices always worked there; this was very necessary, because Rubens had an endless flow of commissions. Without the zealous collaboration of his apprentices, the two thousand paintings and panels attributed to Rubens could never have been done, no matter how productive the painter was himself. In addition, Rubens worked with other Masters such as Jan Bruegel, Paul de Vos and Jordaens, who painted in the backgrounds, still lifes, animals and so on, in his paintings. Rubens had received a commission from the city council of Antwerp immediately upon his return to the city. This was *The Adoration of the Shepherds*, which was intended for the ceremonial hall where the Twelve Years' Truce was to be signed. The painting was still strongly influenced by Italian art, as were the other works which he did in his first years in Antwerp, such as the monumental triptych, *The Raising of the Cross*, dating from 1610. This work for the St. Walburgis Church is a synthesis of everything that he learned in Italy: the broad composition reminiscent of Tintoretto, the plastic representation of figures in the style of Michelangelo, the warm Venetian colours. Rubens added a new dramatic intensity to these elements. The forceful diagonal line in the central canvas was surrounded by a turmoil of distorted bodies. These dynamics were also characteristic of his many mythological paintings such as for example, *The Battle of the Amazons* (1618). A year later, this violent drama was replaced by a more austere clarity. The colours became lighter and cooler, and the background was often neutral in this stylistic stage in his work, which is described as "classical". The masterful *Descent from the Cross* (1612-1614) is a good example of this.

After 1615, Rubens once again used the more dynamic style in wild hunting scenes, mythological subjects and numerous altarpieces which were amongst the rapidly growing commissions. Between 1617 and 1621, Anthonie van Dyck (1599-1641), the most famous apprentice Rubens was ever to have in his studio, also worked on the execution of the large paintings. Some of the commissions were done in the studio on the basis of sketches by Rubens, and he himself painted only the essential parts, such as the faces. Another task of the apprentices was to copy popular paintings and aristocratic portraits which were commissioned by the various European courts. However, Rubens painted the most important works himself. In fact, he did not only paint; he designed title pages and did illustrations for his friend, Balthasar Moretus, the director of the Plantijn printers. He supervised engravers to make prints of his paintings, and also designed carpets, sculptures and architectural ornamentation. This work had a great influence on other branches of art.

THE LARGE SERIES

In about 1620, light colours began to dominate Rubens' work, and he no longer made use of chiaroscuro - which he had used in Italy - to produce the nuances. This stage of his work covers the period from 1620-1628, and could also be described as the period of "the large series". It was a time when Rubens received many commissions for paintings and carpets. In 1620, he was commissioned to do thirty-nine paintings for the new Jesuit Church in Antwerp. With the help of his assistants, he completed this series in less than a year. Unfortunately, it was lost in a fire in 1718, but many of the sketches in oils survived. Two years later, he received a commission for the historical series about the life of Maria de' Medici and Henri IV, (a cycle which was never completed). It was commissioned by Maria de' Medici for her new Paris residence, the Palais du Luxembourg. In the same year, 1622, King Louis XIII commissioned designs for twelve tapestries about the life of the Emperor Constantine, and between 1625 and 1627, Rubens designed twenty patterns for the series of tapestries, *The Triumph of the Eucharist*, which the Governess Isabella commissioned for the monastery of the Descalzas Reales in Madrid. In addition to these large series, Rubens painted a number of altarpieces during this period which constitute the climax of Baroque painting, such as *The Adoration of the Magi*, dating from 1624.

THE PAINTER AS DIPLOMAT

After he had worked in Antwerp almost exclusively for ten years, the years which followed were characterized by a large number of journeys. Many of these were diplomatic missions which Rubens undertook for Isabella from 1623. After the death of Albrecht in 1621, she ruled the Southern Netherlands on her own. Rubens was well educated and enjoyed the good life. He spoke a large number of languages fluently and was extremely suitable for the complicated missions which were aimed at restoring peace between the Southern and Northern Netherlands after the end of the Twelve Years' Truce in 1621, while attempts were also made to conclude a peace treaty between Spain and England.

In his role as a diplomat, Rubens met the Duke of Buckingham in Paris in 1625, with his diplomatic emissary, Balthasar Gerbier; the latter was also a painter with whom he had an excellent relationship. The Duke of Buckingham was not only an influential minister of the English kings, James I and Charles I, but also of one of the greatest art collectors of his time, and he commissioned Rubens to do two large portraits. Diplomatic missions which resulted in commissions for paintings were characteristic of this period in Rubens' life. He was forced to paint less, but he did make some important contacts for his work.

The death of Rubens' wife, Isabella, in 1626 - probably a victim of the plague - was a great blow to him. He was left with two sons, aged twelve and eight. In order to get over his grief, he accepted even more diplomatic missions than before. In 1627, he travelled to Holland to negotiate, and in August 1628, he travelled on an urgent mission to Madrid to report to King Philip IV about his attempts to bring about peace between Spain and England. While he was in the Spanish capital - a stay that lasted for months because of the murder of the most important negotiator, the Duke of Buckingham - he painted portraits of Philip and his family. Philip was so delighted with Rubens' work that in 1636 he commissioned him to paint a series of more than a hundred mythological scenes for his hunting lodge. In addition, after Rubens' death, he bought a large number of paintings which remained in the artist's house. Consequently, Madrid still has one of the largest Rubens collections in the world.

In 1629, Rubens was in London once again on behalf of King Philip to negotiate with Charles I. This eventually led to a peace treaty. On this occasion he painted *Minerva Protects Pax against Mars*, or *War and Peace*, for the king, a clear reference to his negotiation attempts. Before leaving England he accepted an important commission from Charles I to do the paintings for the ceiling of the banqueting hall in the Palace of Whitehall. After returning to Antwerp, Rubens started work on this project and completed it in 1635. During his regular visits to England in this period, Rubens also painted several portraits of prominent Englishmen, such as the Count of Arundel. The way in which Rubens was distinguished for his services reveals how much his royal patrons valued him both as a diplomat and as a painter. In 1624, he was granted a noble title by the King of Spain. In 1630, he was knighted by Charles I, and in 1631 he was knighted by Philip IV. Although Rubens spent a lot of time at the courts of Europe, it did not mean that he liked life at court. He had been hesitant about accepting the position of court painter to Albrecht and Isabella, because he was afraid of having to become a courtier. When he completed the huge commission for Charles I in 1635, he had the paintings taken there by someone else, because he "abhorred life at Court", as he wrote to his friend, the French scholar Nicolas-Claude Fabri de Peiresc.

NEW HAPPINESS

In April 1630, the painter finally returned to Antwerp where he went back to work energetically, despite the fact that he had suffered from gout in his hands for several years. In his studio he worked on a number of large commissions. Apart from the nine paintings for Charles I's banqueting hall, there was a commission for a series of tapestries on the life of Achilles, and the life of Henry IV, which Maria de' Medici wished to have, despite the objections of Cardinal Richelieu. This last project was a source of irritation for Rubens. He had already started on it, when he was suddenly given completely different dimensions by the palace architect, and consequently had to "change, spoil and mutilate" all his designs. He asked for more space and put the work aside, awaiting an answer. Nine months later, Maria de' Medici fled from France after quarrelling with Richelieu, and the commission was cancelled altogether after ten years of negotiations.

At the end of 1630, Rubens, now fifty-three years old, married a woman who was not of noble birth as his friends had advised him, but Hélène Fourment, a beautiful young girl who was not yet seventeen. She was the daughter of his old friend and neighbour, Daniel Fourment, and a niece of his dead wife. His friend, Caspar Gevartius, wrote a Latin poem on this occasion in which he declared that Helena of Antwerp, unlike Helen of Troy, was a perfect woman, in whose arms the greatest of all painters would rediscover his youth. These words proved to be prophetic - Hélène was a source of happiness and inspiration in the last ten years of Rubens' life. Her beauty inspired the painter to make wonderful portraits. She can be recognized in the biblical paintings, and above all, in the mythological works from Rubens' last period.

The painter's last ten years are known as his "lyrical period", and during these years he painted his most intimate work. He did fewer altarpieces. They were no longer completely in the exuberant Baroque style but were more subdued, and they contain far fewer figures. It was as though Rubens had decided to concentrate on his favourite subjects, and he painted them mainly on canvases and panels of a fairly modest size. His favourite subjects included mythology, and he depicted the themes against a background of Arcadian landscapes in which the almost transparent naked nymphs and cupids are like an ode to sensual delight.

FAREWELL TO DIPLOMACY

After his second marriage, Rubens wished to withdraw from his diplomatic role, but Isabella found it difficult to do without the services of her confidant, and in 1631 she sent him on a difficult mission concerning Maria de' Medici. The intrigues of the Queen Mother of France against Richelieu had failed, and she fled to the Netherlands where Rubens was instructed to welcome her on behalf of the Archduchess. Maria told him that she was preparing a rebellion in her country to topple Richelieu, led by her younger son, the Duke of Orleans, and that she only needed the financial support of Spain. As a peace-loving man, Rubens was undoubtedly not very positive about this plan, but Richelieu was a dangerous enemy of Spain, and for that reason the painter-diplomat insisted that the Spanish court support the rebellion. Maria de' Medici's conspiracy came to nothing, and in the spring of 1632, Rubens begged the Archduchess to relieve him of these missions in future. She did absolve him from the obligation to become involved with Maria de' Medici's intrigues, but she continued to send him on peace missions to the Prince of Orange. There was an urgent need for a truce with Holland, because Spain was not giving any financial support, and the war was going badly for the Spanish Netherlands, where the people had had more than enough of the lengthy war. Rubens agreed to continue his confidential negotiations in the hope of peace. He acted from a sense of loyalty to the Archduchess, the lawful ruler, but this placed him in a difficult position among his compatriots, who felt that he placed Spanish interests above those of their own country. They wished for official negotiations with the States of Holland, and did not appreciate the private interviews with the Prince of Orange. The leader of the official delegation which was to negotiate in The Hague, the Duke of Aerschot, did not accept Rubens as an independent delegate and required him to report to him. In a rather undiplomatic letter, Rubens refused to do so, and the Duke responded with a public insult. The Duke's insulting behaviour towards the painter who had brought so much fame to his country, embarrassed even his critics and unexpectedly led to Rubens' great popularity being restored. The Archduchess Isabella died at the end of 1633, and Rubens withdrew from politics for ever.

In 1634, Antwerp started on the preparations for the Triumphal Inauguration of Isabella's successor, the Cardinal-Infant Ferdinand, and the city council asked Rubens to design the triumphal arches, the triumphal chariot and other decorations. Rubens delighted in this commission and designed arches and galleries of pillars in an impressive Baroque style. On the basis of Rubens' sketches, a large group of Antwerp painters painted the canvases to decorate the arches, but the master himself also worked on the project so that everything would be ready on time.

When Ferdinand officially entered Antwerp in April 1635, Rubens was too ill to join in the celebrations, but the ruler visited him at home to thank him for his work. This indicated the great status which the painter had, a status which is also revealed in the self-portrait which he painted in about 1635 in which he shows himself as a nobleman with his hand on the blade of his dagger.

THE LAST GREAT COMMISSION

In the same year, Rubens bought the estate, Het Steen, where he spent the summers with his new family, which now included three children. In these rural surroundings he painted more landscapes than he had ever done before, inspired by the beautiful and luxuriant environment. From 1636-1638, he worked in his studio in Antwerp on the largest commission he ever received. This was a series of more than a hundred and twenty panels based on the stories from Ovid's *Metamorphoses*, which was intended for Philip IV's hunting lodge, Torre de la Parada. Only four of the paintings were done by Rubens himself; the others were executed on the basis of his sketches in oils by leading Antwerp painters, such as Jacob Jordeans, Cornelis de Vos, and Erasmus Quellin. The sketches are amongst Rubens' best work, despite the fact that he was increasingly tortured by rheumatic pains in his hands (often described as "gout") which meant that he was sometimes even unable to hold a brush.

In the autumn of 1638, Rubens fell seriously ill, and in December he was given the Last Sacraments because the doctors feared for his life. However, he recovered, and the following year he was back hard at work. In March 1640, the pains were worse than ever and he could hardly use his right hand. However, this did not prevent him from accepting a commission from Charles I for a Cupid and Psyche. The price for this work, which was never executed, was definitely agreed upon a few days before his death.

In April, the painter was planning to go to his estate, and he worked on the completion of *Perseus and Andromeda* for the King of Spain. He also had a new commission for an altarpiece for a church in Cologne, but on 30 May, Balthasar Gerbier wrote to a friend from Brussels: "Sir Peter Rubens is fatally ill, the doctors of this city have been called to him to help him if they can". The doctors from Brussels came too late and, after a very short illness, Rubens died that evening, almost sixty-three years old.

A few years after his death, as Rubens had requested on his deathbed, *The Madonna with the Saints*, one of his last paintings, was placed above the altar of the commemoration chapel in the St. James' Church, where he is buried. No one could have thought of a more noble or modest commemoration for this painter of genius, who left us a heritage of about two thousand works. His work determined an entire era, and inspired and influenced countless painters of future generations.

Self-portrait (at approximately 60 years old), c. 1636
Canvas, 109.5 x 85 cm
Vienna, Kunsthistorisches Museum

Rubens painted this elegant self-portrait several years before his death. It is the picture of a prosperous, self-assured and intelligent man, who seems to have changed remarkably little since his self-portrait as a bridegroom, dating from 1609.

Rubens and Isabella Brant
under a Honeysuckle
Bower, c. 1609
Canvas, 178 x 136 cm
Munich, Alte Pinakothek

The two right hands placed one on the other indicate that this is a portrait for a marriage, probably painted shortly after the artist's marriage to the eighteen-year-old Isabella, who died in 1623.

The Fall (Adam and Eve), before 1600
Panel, 180 x 158 cm
Antwerp, Rubenshuis

This is the most important work painted by the young Rubens before he travelled to Italy. The influence of the style of one of his teachers, Otto van Veen (or Vaenius) is clearly visible. An engraving by Marcantonio Raimondi served as an example for the subject of this painting.

The Descent from the Cross, 1612-14
Middle panel, 418 x 310 cm, side panel, 418 x 149.5 cm
Antwerp, Cathedral of Our Lady

At the end of 1611 the Arquebusiers' Guild commissioned this large triptych, which shows
the patron saint of the guild, St. Christopher, with the Christ child on his shoulders, on the
back of the panels.
The monumental central panel is flanked by "The Visitation of Mary" (on the left), and "the
Presentation in the Temple" (on the right). There is a striking change to a lighter and cooler range
of colours in this composition which draws the viewer's eye towards the figure of Christ.

The Elevation of the Cross, c. 1610
Panel, 459 x 339 cm
Antwerp, Cathedral of Our Lady

This is the central panel of a triptych which is one of the most famous and important works from this
period. Rubens painted it for the St. Walburg Church in Antwerp, and it was his first commission for
an altarpiece in that city. The warm colours and strong contrasts between light and shadow in this
powerful painting are reminiscent of Tintoretto, whose work Rubens had studied in Venice.

The Hunt on the Hippopotamus and the Crocodile, 1615-1616
Canvas, 247 x 321 cm
Munich, Alte Pinakothek

This extremely original and suggestive work formed part of a series of four hunting scenes commissioned by Duke Maximilian of Bavaria for Schleissheim Castle. The series also included "The Hunt on the Wild Boar", "The Hunt on the Lion, the Leopard and the Tiger", and "The Hunt on Lions", and probably referred to the four continents symbolised by their most characteristic animals. These works had a great influence on 19th century French painters.

The Hunt on the Hippopotamus and the Crocodile, (detail)

Juno and Argus, c. 1611, canvas, 255 x 348 cm
Cologne, Wallraf-Richartz-Museum

One of the many mythological works painted by Rubens during the years after his return from Italy.
The peacock's tail refers to the hundred eyes of the monster Argus. His hewn off head lies in the lap
of the young woman next to Juno, who shows the girl handfuls of eyes.

Madonna with Child within a Garland of Flowers, 1616-18, panel, 158 x 210 cm
Munich, Alte Pinakothek

The garland of flowers in this painting, composed as a medallion, was painted by Jan Bruegel the
Elder, who worked with Rubens a great deal during these years.

The Garland of Fruit, c. 1616, canvas, 120 x 203 cm
Munich, Alte Pinakothek

The "putti" (literally "chaps" in Italian), which also surround the "Madonna with Child within a
Garland of Flowers", are based on the god Amor, and were incorporated as playful elements in
painting and sculpture from the time of the Renaissance.

The Abduction of the Daughters of Leukyppos, c. 1616
Canvas, 222 x 209 cm
Munich, Alte Pinakothek

Rubens' skill in representing the human skin is particularly clear in this depiction of the abduction of two nymphs by the demigods, Castor and Pollux.

The Hermit and the Sleeping Angelica, 1626-28
Panel, 48 x 66 cm
Vienna, Kunsthistorisches Museum

The old hermit is seriously tempted by the naked, sleeping beauty, who remains totally unaware, while a devilish figure looks on curiously, waiting for the moment when the old man starts to sin.

The (small) Last Judgement, c. 1620
Canvas, 183.5 x 119 cm
Munich, Alte Pinakothek

In a desperate whirlwind of intertwined bodies, the damned crash down to hell, chased by harnessed angels. In the background, above the welter of bodies, the Supreme Judge surveys the scene with the Virgin Mary at His side.

The (small) Last Judgement, (detail)

The Battle of the Amazons, c. 1616-18
Panel, 121 x 165.5 cm
Munich, Alte Pinakothek

The battle on the bridge is a quotation from Leonardo's "Battle of Anghiari", a work which was lost, and is known mainly from copies made by Rubens. The panel also contains references to antique sarcophagi on which this battle is often depicted.

Arrival of Maria de' Medici in Marseille, 1622-25
Panel, 63.7 x 50 cm
Munich, Alte Pinakothek

This small panel - also known as "Disembarkation in Marseille" - was a preliminary study for a large work (see p. 32) which formed part of a cycle about the life of the French queen. The Queen, the mother of Louis XIII, commissioned the 20 works from Rubens in 1622 for her new Paris residence, the Palais du Luxembourg. The painting, "The Capture of Gulik", shown on p. 33, is the fifteenth work in this series.

Arrival of Maria de' Medici in Marseille, 1622-25
Canvas, 394 x 295, Paris, The Louvre

The Capture of Gulik, 1622-25
Canvas, 394 x 295 cm, Paris, The Louvre

The Flight of St. Barbara, c. 1620
Panel, 32 x 46.5 cm
London, Dulwich College Picture Gallery

A beautiful small panel in the Italian style which is particularly dynamic because of the perspective from below.

Adoration of the Magi, 1624
Panel, 447 x 336 cm
Antwerp, Royal Museum for Fine Arts

Only the ox in the foreground seems uninterested in the Christ child in this impressive "Adoration". All eyes, even those of the camel in the background, are focused on the child, who innocently enjoys the attention, despite the intensity of their gaze. This intensity even seems to draw the viewer's eye to the object of the adoration.

Brigida Spinola Doria, 1606
Canvas, 152 x 99 cm
Washington, National
Gallery of Art,
Samuel H. Kress Collection

This portrait of the marquess is one of the nine splendid portraits of the Genoese nobility which Rubens painted in the years 1606-07.
The series indicated a new development in official seventeenth century portrait painting. The painting, which originally showed the whole figure, was cut away at the bottom so that the signature and date were removed.

Caspar Gevartius, 1630, panel, 119 x 98 cm
Antwerp, Royal Museum for Fine Arts

Head of a Young Girl
(Clara Serena Rubens?), c. 1616
Panel, 37 x 27 cm
Vaduz, Fürstlich Liechtenstein'sche
Gemäldegalerie

Although it is not entirely certain, it is generally assumed that this famous small portrait is of the artist's oldest daughter, who was born in 1611 and died in 1623.

Suzanna Fourment, c. 1625, canvas, 79 x 55 cm
London, National Gallery

Suzanna was the eldest daughter of the merchant, Daniel Fourment, a good friend of Rubens. The young woman was painted many times, both by Anthonie van Dyck and by Rubens, but this portrait, also known by the title, "Chapeau de Paille" (or "The Straw Hat"), is undoubtedly the best and most famous.

The Assumption of Mary, c. 1626, panel, 506 x 321 cm
Antwerp, Cathedral of Our Lady

The Ascent of Calvary, 1634-38, canvas, 568 x 335 cm
Brussels, Royal Museum for Fine Arts

The Centaur Chiron Instructs the Young Achilles, 1630-32
Panel, 43 x 36.5 cm
Rotterdam, Boymans - van Beuningen Museum

Achilles with the Daughters of Lycomedes, 1630-32
Panel, 45.5 x 61.5 cm
Rotterdam, Boymans - van Beuningen Museum

The panels on these two pages were studies for a series of tapestries about the life of the
Greek hero, Achilles, the son of the sea nymph, Thetis, who had rendered him invulnerable
by submerging him in the river of the dead, the Styx.
Only his heel, where she had held onto him, remained vulnerable until his downfall.

The Castle Gardens of Het Steen, 1635-40
Panel, 52.7 x 97 cm
Vienna, Kunsthistorisches Museum

In 1635 Rubens bought the estate, Het Steen, situated about twenty miles south of Antwerp.
He painted there for his own pleasure, without the pressure of his patrons. These late works were the most personal and lightest landscapes.

The Castle Gardens of Het Steen (detail)

The Judgement of Paris, 1632-35, panel, 145 x 194 cm
London, National Gallery

This version of the famous mythological subject was commissioned by King Philip IV of Spain. The king was told in confidence that the naked Venus in the work was the painter's wife, "who was undoubtedly the most beautiful woman in the country at that time". It is actually not certain whether Rubens really did use his second wife, the young Hélène Fourment, as a model.

The Triumphal Chariot of Calloo, c. 1638, panel, 103 x 71 cm
Antwerp, Royal Museum of Fine Arts

After the Cardinal-Infant Ferdinand had won a victory over the Dutch for the Spanish Netherlands at Calloo, Antwerp welcomed him with festivities.
Rubens designed the decorations; for example, this triumphal chariot with figures representing the City, the Victory, Triumph, Virtue and Happiness, with two bound prisoners between them. The chariot was such a success that it was used for decades for the annual processions in Antwerp.

Hélène Fourment in a Bridal Dress, 1630-31, panel, 160 x 134 cm, Munich, Alte Pinakothek
Rubens remarried in 1630; his bride was Hélène Fourment, who was 16 years old at the time.

The Fur Cloak, c. 1638
Panel, 176 x 83 cm
Vienna, Kunsthistorisches
Museum

Rubens painted this intimate
portrait of his second wife for
himself, and left it to her so
that it would stay in the
family.

Hélène Fourment with her children, 1636-37, panel, 113 x 82 cm
Paris, The Louvre
A light and tender impression of Rubens' second family.

The Three Graces, c. 1638-40
Panel, 221 x 181 cm
Madrid, The Prado

Diana and Callisto, c. 1638-40, canvas, 202 x 323 cm
Madrid, The Prado

The Flemish Fair, c. 1636
Panel, 149 x 261 cm
Paris, The Louvre

During his travels through the areas around Het Steen, Rubens came into contact with life in the countryside and in villages which had been depicted by Pieter Bruegel, Rubens painted the exuberance and excesses of the "kermesse", the annual village feast, with baroque exaggeration, so that the scene transcends reality. It is as much a personal interpretation of this subject as the mythological works shown on the page on the left.

The Judgement of Paris, c. 1638-39
Canvas, 199 x 372 cm
Madrid, The Prado

The Fall of Icarus, 1636-38
Panel, 27 x 27 cm
Brussels, Royal Museum of Fine Arts

The Abduction of Hippodameia, c. 1636-38
Panel, 26 x 40 cm
Brussels, Royal Museum of Fine Arts

Philip IV, who was an enthusiastic collector of Rubens' work, commissioned the artist in 1636 to paint a large series of works for the hunting lodge, Torre de la Parada, near Madrid. The cycle, one of the largest projects Rubens accepted in his later years, illustrated mythological scenes from Ovid's "Metamorphoses". Some of the subject Rubens chose were almost "obligatory", such as "The Fall of Icarus", but he also used a number of the most cruel and bloody scenes as a starting point, perhaps as a silent comment on the violent age in which he lived. He completed the commission in March 1638, and no fewer that 112 panels were shipped to Spain.

Madonna with the Saints, c. 1638-40, panel, 211 x 195 cm
Antwerp, St. Jacob's Church

Rubens intended one of the last altarpieces which he made for his own tomb in the
St. Jacob's Church in Antwerp, where it can still be seen.